GW00726064

THE MYSTERIOUS SCORPIO

Text by Therrie Rosenvald

Illustrations and Design by Marco Schmidt

Copyright © Therrie Rosenvald & Marco Schmidt 2004, 2009

All rights reserved. No part of this publication may be reproduced, stored in or introduced into a retrieval system, or transmitted in any form or by any means (electronic, mechanical, photocopying, recording or otherwise) without written permission of the publisher. Any person who does any unauthorised act in relation to this publication may be liable to criminal prosecution and civil claims for damages.

3rd Edition 2009
2nd Edition 2004
1st Edition 2001

ISBN 10 Digit: 1-877063-07-X

ISBN 13 Digit: 978-1-877063-07-7

Published by
Astrology Art
24 Wallace Road
Beachmere 4510
Queensland, Australia

www.astrologyart.com.au

CONTENTS

THE FASCINATING SCORPIO

Scorpio is probably the least understood sign of the Zodiac. As much as they like to uncover the skeletons in other people's closets, Scorpios themselves are very secretive. Getting to know them is not an easy task. Scorpios rarely divulge their most secret thoughts. If they do share a bit of themselves with others it is usually with an ulterior motive. Even after years of friendship - or marriage - Scorpios often remain a mystery to those close to them, and that's how they like it.

Their above average perception allows Scorpios to see deep into the souls of their fellow man, which is why it is often rumored that Scorpios possess dark magical powers or are in cahoots with the spirits from beyond. With their hypnotic stare Scorpios are masters at drawing out the most hidden secrets of anyone and delving into the murky waters of other people's emotions is one of their favorite hobbies, which is why Scorpio is considered to be the sign of psychotherapists.

The planet associated with Scorpio is Pluto, the ancient God of the Underworld. This explains why most Scorpios are irresistibly drawn to the sleazy areas of the city, where they can study the darkest corners of human nature. Scorpio has no sentimental illusions about mankind and is only too well aware that both good and evil reign in the human heart. There is absolutely nothing that will shock a Scorpio. Death also falls into the realms of Scorpio and it is said that Scorpios would rather self-destruct than be controlled by an outside force.

The Scorpio element is water and the term "still waters run deep" certainly applies to this sign. Actually, every description of Scorpio emphasizes the depth of their passion. But their passion doesn't just refer to their sexual drive, Scorpios are passionate about everything, their work, their hobbies, their families, they are even passionate about their enemies. To the outside world Scorpios usually display a cool facade, but underneath the emotions are boiling like the lava in a volcano.

Getting on the wrong side of Scorpios can be very painful. The Scorpio sting, be it verbal or otherwise, is devastating, if not deadly. These people will take revenge for any wrongdoing not only once, but again and again. Scorpios never forget and once someone has disappointed them, it's nearly impossible to get back into the good books with them.

Scorpio is one of the most powerful signs of the Zodiac. Their strength lies in their ability to look at themselves honestly. They are determined to overcome weaknesses and turn them into strengths. This has given Scorpios the skills to quickly ferret out the weaknesses in others and use these for their own purpose. They will use every trick in the book to get what they want. Scorpios are complex and intense people. Their desires and longings sometimes take over and they become quite brazen in the pursuit of their goals. Their inner depth energizes them and if this force can be channeled properly it gives them great qualities of endurance and they will battle against enormous odds and win. If they have to trample on a few feet in the process, well that can't be helped.

But the inner strength and passion of this sign can also be a two-edged sword. It can destroy just as expertly and swiftly as it can defend. Sometimes the eagle is also used as a symbol for this sign, which highlights the power with which they swoop upon their prey. Scorpios must themselves become aware of the force within and learn to respect it and direct it for the good of all.

Scorpios always succeed at whatever they undertake. If the object of their desire is turning out to be elusive, be it a career or a person, they are not disheartened. Quite the opposite is true; they become more single-minded and pursue their goal with increased vigor. Scorpios have great personal magnetism and they are enshrouded by mystery, which makes them extremely fascinating. Scorpios live their life on their terms alone.

SEDUCTIVE AND DANGEROUS

She's alluring, she's sensuous and she is a mystery. She'll beguile you with her intuition and femininity. With her hypnotic powers she'll make you believe that she is the softest and most demure creature that ever walked this earth. Until you upset her. Then this gentle creature will suddenly turn into a fire-spitting dragon and the pain of her verbal stings lasts a very long time. The Scorpio female is no plaything. The man who treats her with disrespect and injures her fierce pride will quickly and deeply regret it.

Trying to understand the Scorpio woman is like trying to understand the mysteries of the universe. Just when you're sure that you've uncovered all sides to this mystifying creature, she'll transform herself right before your eyes into something new. She's the femme fatale, willing to live out your wildest fantasies and some of her own, which will surpass yours in terms of earthiness. Or she may pretend to be Dorothy from the Wizard of Oz, all innocence. Don't believe it, there is nothing innocent about a Scorpio. Given half a chance Ms Scorpio will twist and turn your emotions in any direction she pleases, and enjoy it too.

The Scorpio female is no fool and knows exactly what she wants in life. This girl is passionate about everything, love, life, her dog and her lover. She won't accept weakness in herself or in others. She has high expectations of those she loves and she will urge them to face their failings with the same tenacity that she tries to turn her own perceived flaws into strengths. She is not easily impressed and winning her heart will be quite a feat. Though she loves the obscure and a slanted, sarcastic sense of humor or any outrageous suggestions will generally win her over.

Her honest judgments might at times seem cruel and devastating, but they are always accurate. She can't abide hypocrites and will see through any deception in seconds. The Scorpio woman admires strength of character and strength of mind. She is not for the timid, but she's the most exciting and tantalizing woman you will ever meet.

PASSIONATE TO THE EXTREME

When meeting a Scorpio male one immediately thinks of danger and passion. If passion in every sense of the word makes you uneasy it would be wise to make your exit now. Don't be fooled by the calm gaze and the seemingly placid nature. Look again. The gaze may be serene, but it penetrates your soul and the placid composure is the result of skilled self-control.

When Mr Scorpio has hypnotized you with his magnetic powers and brought you under his spell, you'll soon discover that there is nothing placid about this man. But then it's already too late for an escape. He will make your head spin and with his analytical mind he will penetrate to the core of your inner being. Trying to hide anything from the Scorpio male is a waste of time.

If you're a bit of daredevil yourself and danger excites you, you couldn't have found a better match. The Scorpio male will take your heart, your soul, your mind and your body and stir up emotions you didn't know existed. This is no ordinary man. At times he may want to chain you to his lair, at other times he'll brood in a corner and pretend you don't exist. But if you're loyal to him he will lay the world at your feet and give his life for your love. Be warned though, this is not a man to trifle with. He is fiercely proud and jealous. So don't even think about playing with fire, because that barb at the end of his tail is deadly.

Although the Scorpio's natural habitat is the desert this is a water sign and therefore the emotions are deep and plentiful. Scorpio men are never shallow; it's either boiling hot or icy cold. This is definitely not a man you want to antagonize because not only is his wrath long-lasting; his retributions are usually drawn out and excruciatingly painful. He can have a bit of a sadistic and even a masochistic streak, as he will not hesitate to forfeit his own well-being just to make a point. But life with a Scorpio man will be exhilarating on a spiritual and physical level. His sexual stamina is legendary. This is a man who does nothing by half measures; it's all or nothing for him.

TO WIN AT ALL COSTS

To define Scorpio's idea of success is rather difficult as they are very cagey about their intentions and aspirations. Success can also be different for each one of them. For some it may be becoming chairman of a major corporation, for others it may be making a scientific discovery or winning a sports event. For a few it may be as simple as settling a score with an old adversary. Whatever it is, there is no doubt that Scorpio will succeed by whatever means necessary.

When it comes to fulfilling their ambitions Scorpios are ruthless. Anyone thinking they can get in Scorpio's way will soon regret the decision. On their road to success Scorpios leave a long trail of broken spirits in their wake. Once at the top they certainly make a formidable impression, but their secretive nature becomes even more pronounced and they guard their position jealously.

For Scorpios the material rewards are not the primary motivation, neither is the status of being the boss. Sometimes they embark on a personal competition with someone they don't like. For lack of a worthy adversary Scorpios may even compete against themselves. Scorpios must win at all costs, even if they don't care about the prize. Being second best at anything is definitely not good enough for them.

Scorpios harbor secret ambitions that one day they will understand the forces of good and evil. They fearlessly enter areas others don't even want to acknowledge that they exist. Uncovering the mysteries of spirituality, pealing back the layers of human nature and exposing the raw emotions and deep-rooted fears and inhibitions of their adversaries, is something they could strive for.

Scorpios have an unquenchable thirst for power, and in their view knowledge is power. Therefore Scorpios will go to extraordinary lengths to find out all of their opponent's secrets. Some sordid little scandal may be just the right ammunition for the fatal blow.

LOVE MATCH SCORPIO AND SCORPIO

When two Scorpios join together it can either bring out the best or the worst in them. Both are intense, demanding and have a tendency to become obsessed. Just as they are capable of a very deep love and be blissfully happy together, if things go wrong their animosity is just as potent and there is a good chance that they may end up destroying each other. But they respect each other's strength and will find release for their powerful emotions in their sex life. On the positive side, this couple has the ability to explore the universe, uncover the deepest secrets of the soul and reach dimensions that are beyond mere mortals. This is a relationship based on all the senses.

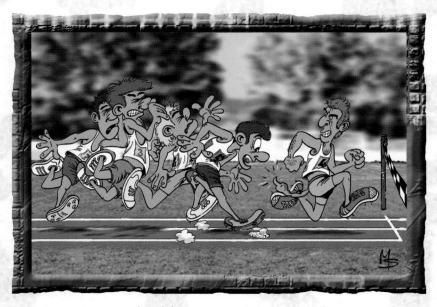

Scorpios are highly competitive and they won't hesitate to use all means at their disposal to hold off any rivals and ensure they achieve their goal.

SEXY AND INTIMIDATING

When trying to describe the impressions Scorpios make with their appearance, the words 'cloak and dagger' come to mind. It is not difficult to picture the male Scorpio as the deadly Count Dracula and the female as his bloodthirsty, beguiling vampire. Anything to do with Scorpios is never going to be meek and mild and this applies just as much to their dress style as to their personality. They enjoy using their outward appearance to shock, confuse and sometimes even to intimidate others. Scorpio's appearance always spells out 'don't mess with me' and 'keep your distance if you want to keep your head'.

The Scorpio style is more suggestive than actually revealing. No one can carry off that sexy, slightly decadent look as masterly as Scorpios without appearing cheap or vulgar. In general, Scorpios don't care much about fashion. They instinctively know what suits them and what doesn't. No matter what they wear, they always manage to look stylish and elegant. Scorpios often forgo jewelry altogether or only wear a small item. The typical Scorpio style is laid back and subtle with simple, clean, classical lines, which accentuate their sensuous nature.

Scorpios are loners and very secretive. Their inner mood will seldom be reflected in their outfits. However, their deep sensuality comes through loud and clear and their strong sex appeal is all too visible. With the burgundy color of a heavy, intoxicating wine, they seduce their prey. With the dark blue shades of the deep ocean, they lure them into their cave and take possession of their minds. With the purple and black of luscious grapes, they devour their victim very slowly.

Anyone hoping to discover more about the Scorpio character by viewing their home will be disappointed. The Scorpio home is as mysterious and secretive as they are themselves. It will be elegant in a simplistic, yet functional way. A few choice pieces create the overall atmosphere of seduction and clever lighting sets the scene for whatever is to come. The Scorpio lair is hard to escape from.

LOVE MATCH SCORPIO AND SAGITTARIUS

Sagittarius' uninhibited manner will fascinate Scorpio. But this union will not always be smooth. Restless and wild Sagittarius doesn't like to be controlled. Also Sagittarius is casual about things of the heart, whereas the emotional bonding is sacred to Scorpio. Scorpio must watch the possessiveness and jealousy. Sagittarius is a free spirit. However, Scorpio will be the strength Sagittarius can lean on when things get muddled up a bit, which they invariably do when Sagittarius has his or her fingers in the pie. But Sagittarius is the ultimate optimist and will always be able to draw Scorpio out of the brooding mood. Also Sagittarius is a willing partner in the most outrageous bedroom antics.

Scorpios get a real kick out of shocking
other people. They take the idea of
power dressing to a whole new level.

MANIPULATIVE & POWER HUNGRY

When it comes to power Scorpios are definitely at the top of the tree. The mental, physical and emotional power and passion they bring to their careers or professions are second to none. Once Scorpios inject a project with their volcanic energies it is bound to light up the sky. Scorpios are intense and never lose sight of their goals. They are manipulative and very patient. They can bide their time and wait for the perfect moment to make a move, and that move will be precise, on target and deadly.

In business Scorpios are tenacious competitors with an extraordinary determination. As employees they are responsible, imaginative and very thorough in their work. They neither need nor do they like control. In fact, controlling others is something Scorpios usually do and are very good at. Giving them snide orders, or talking down to them is not always a good idea. Sooner or later Scorpios climb the corporate ladder and often end up taking over the company or at least becoming the boss and they have very long memories and can be slightly vindictive.

Their superior sensitivity and the ability to see beyond the surface often lead Scorpios onto career paths that involve the human psyche. The most repugnant tales will not distress Scorpio. They are really in their element as psychotherapists, psychologists and prison wardens or detectives. With their x-ray vision they soon uncover hidden secrets and can rattle long forgotten skeletons in anyone's closet. If they go bad, they make highly successful criminals. They will devise devious, sophisticated plots and plan their clandestine activities to the minutest detail.

As employers Scorpios are strict taskmasters, but fair. They usually are devoted to their work and expect the same level of commitment from their staff. They have the tendency to stretch the endurance and abilities of their workforce to the limit. They show respect and expect respect and their orders are carved in stone. Competitors will soon take notice of them. Their tactics are ruthless and the odd casualty is of no consequence to them.

LOVE MATCH SCORPIO AND CAPRICORN

Both Scorpio and Capricorn approach matters of the heart with extreme caution. Neither finds it easy to trust others. Therefore their relationship will take a while to get going and they start feeling comfortable with each other. Capricorn considers the strong passions, inner strengths and power of Scorpio as valuable virtues. The infamous Scorpio jealousy will make Capricorn feel secure in the relationship. However, the goat will respond with drawn out brooding to the explosive and volatile emotional outbreaks Scorpio displays occasionally. Otherwise this couple has a purpose in life and both possess enough ambition, determination and maturity to reach their joint goals.

Scorpios spot weaknesses in others in seconds and won't hesitate to manipulate people and circumstances very skillfully to enhance their own position and prospects.

THE GENTLE SIDE OF SCORPIO

The legendary Scorpio passion is even more pronounced when it concerns their children. The love Scorpio parents feel for their children surpasses all other loves, except maybe that for their spouse if they are happily married. They take an active part in every stage of their child's development and channel a great deal of emotional energy into the care of the youngsters. Scorpios will hardly ever miss a school play or a football match. They will be the first to confront the parents of the schoolyard bully. If they feel their child is not getting the education they expected, and paid for, or the child has been unfairly treated, Scorpio parents will take immediate action.

As a water sign, Scorpios make very intuitive parents. They sense when things are not right with their youngsters and will quiz them mercilessly until they uncover the reason for the anguish. Scorpio parents give little Lucy loving support and ease the grieving process when the cat has eaten the goldfish. They will also be there with their inner strength when Tommy doesn't make the grade for the football team. Scorpios quietly offer a shoulder to cry on when the young heart gets broken for the first time.

The downside of their protectiveness is that Scorpios overdo it a bit. They have a tendency to become too controlling and possessive. The young man, who wants to take Scorpio's daughter to the dance, will have to submit to an intensive interrogation about his intentions, family background and character before he is reluctantly given permission. If the poor fellow still has the nerve to bring the girl home one second late, he can forget about ever becoming part of the family.

Scorpios are passionately attached to their children and won't take kindly to relinquishing their son or daughter's heart for the sake of some person they hardly know. However, the happiness of their children is their first priority, and they will grudgingly accept that their babies are grown-up now and can build their own future and experience their own successes and failures.

LOVE MATCH SCORPIO AND AQUARIUS

Scorpio admires the Aquarian commitment to humanitarian causes and is one of the few signs not put off by the Aquarian eccentricity. On the contrary, Scorpio will be highly amused by the antics Aquarius employs in an effort to change the world and thereby usually ends up shocking or offending everybody. No matter how outrageous Aquarius becomes Scorpio lends support when all others criticize. But Aquarius must take care not overdo it with the outside interests. If Aquarius spends too much time away from the home he or she will quickly feel the Scorpio sting. Scorpio has a jealous nature and is not willing to share, even with a good cause.

Scorpios don't mind giving up their time or dignity for the sake of their children. They know that the love and attention they invest in their offspring's childhood will pay off in the child's adulthood.

A FRIEND IN NEED

Having a Scorpio as a friend is not only a great privilege, but also an asset. Scorpios will be at their friend's side when everyone else abandons them. There isn't a scandal large enough or a misfortune big enough to entice Scorpios to drop their friends. But Scorpios do expect that their loyalty be returned.

They will fight tooth and nail for the rights of their friends and will not hesitate to sacrifice their own safety, if the need arises. Scorpios are the ones who donate a kidney to save their friend's life, and will probably insist that they remain anonymous. Being given credit for their generosity and good deeds is not important to Scorpios. The only thing that counts is that someone needed help and Scorpio was able to provide it. Giving a kidney may be a bit extreme, but then extreme is one of Scorpio's most pronounced characteristics.

Becoming Scorpio's friend is not an easy task. Scorpios thoroughly scrutinize the background of any potential friend and they have a way of getting other people to divulge their most sensitive secrets. Someone who cross-dresses or has had a sex change does not put off Scorpios. But they do frown upon disloyalty, gossips and unreliable people. Trust is an important issue for Scorpios. Friends who go blabbing about Scorpio's private affairs will get crossed off the Christmas list very quickly.

Scorpios also don't appreciate it if their friendship is taken for granted or belittled. If they get stood up for anything less than a life-threatening emergency more than once they are unlikely to pursue the friendship further. Actually, over the next few years, every time when Scorpios see that person they might stick that Scorpio barb into their backside, just so they never forget their transgression. Scorpios may outwardly forgive a wrongdoing by a friend, but this is a sign with a deep need for revenge. A friendship with Scorpios can be a bit strenuous as they expect total commitment and loyalty. Usually, Scorpios have only a handful of friends, but these will be very close and long standing.

LOVE MATCH SCORPIO AND PISCES

Scorpio's strength and clear direction coupled with intuition and sensitivity must seem to Pisces like a dream come true. Pisces will only be too happy to surrender to the Scorpio will and give devotion and admiration to the strong protector. Though at times Pisces will be off with the fairies and may be emotionally unavailable. Scorpio is not used to being ignored and may swipe back a bit too brutal. Both being water signs it will take time to forgive and forget. But Scorpio will be able to pull out all the hidden passions and desires in Pisces and their mutual fascination will create a romantic aura. Pisces' flair for the bizarre will continually delight Scorpio.

Just when you thought you were all alone in your predicament your Scorpio friend appears at your side and gives support in big and small ways.

EMOTIONAL TURBULENCES

With Scorpio it is always all or nothing. They are either indulging in physical excesses or they are advocating total abstinence. Scorpios represent the extremes of human emotions, such as love, hatred, generosity, malice, reward and retribution. They don't hold grudges like Cancerians, but if they feel they have been ill-treated it will vex them until they get a chance to even the score. Scorpios are capable of paying back any wrongdoing decades later.

Scorpios rule the sexual organs and their ailments are often of a sexual nature or closely associated. Repressing their feelings and desires can lead to acute stress. Although Scorpios are attuned to their emotions, sometimes the intensity is overwhelming. If they have no outlet for their tensions they will experience problems in their lower back and general discomfort in the reproductive organs, especially in women. Feeling frustrated doesn't improve their mood either.

Their intense emotions do often become their biggest hurdle to overcome. Scorpios would rather feel unhappy than feel nothing at all. They are also prone to psychosomatic complaints. Relaxation techniques, a healthy diet, regular exercise and a moderate lifestyle help Scorpios to rid themselves of the emotional and physical toxins on a regular basis.

However, Scorpios are very resilient. Although they burn their candles at both ends most of the time, even when sick, it is often astounding how fast they recuperate. Whereas others need months to overcome serious illnesses, Scorpios are out and about in a matter of days. They can bounce back virtually from the brink of death without an ill effect. Scorpio represents the House of Death and Rebirth, which might give some clue to this astounding phenomenon. In mythology everything that dies is reborn in a different form. This may explain why Scorpios are so casual about their own safety, actually it often seems as if they go out of their way to taunt fate and ultimately death.

LOVE MATCH SCORPIO AND ARIES

The physical attraction is strong. With Scorpio Arians can experiment to their heart's content, especially in bed. But there will be some trouble when it comes to decision-making. Both are used to getting their own way. Scorpio won't accept the Arian quest for freedom quietly. Also Aries should try to stop flirting with everybody within shouting range. Arians are often too caught up in themselves to notice when their behavior is hurting their partner. Scorpios won't take a back seat or tolerate being shoved aside. When the fury explodes between these two it is not a pretty sight. Just as well Aries doesn't hold any grudges. This couple would do best to learn to share the power.

Scorpios have an open mind regarding the use of alternative medicines. Brewing weird potions to shield off negative influences may just be the secret to their physical and mental resilience.

DRAWN TO THE UNDERWORLD

Scorpio holidays are not holidays in the traditional sense. They rarely include relaxing on the beach or visiting well-known tourist spots. While others enjoy the view of Paris from the top of the Eiffel Tower, Scorpios will be seeking out the red-light district and the seedy side of the city. As they are ruled by Pluto, the God of the Underworld, they have a particular interest in immorality and decay. Observing mankind at its worst fascinates Scorpios.

Scorpios just love intriguing and mysterious destinations. They won't think twice about traveling to Transylvania in search of Dracula's castle. If it is infamous and obscure Scorpios will want to discover it. They would travel into the deepest jungles and marshes, put up with snakes and other venomous creepy-crawlies, to get to an ancient tribe and learn the secrets of their dark magical powers. Travel is a tool for Scorpios to discover the essence of strange cultures and to learn more about themselves and their inner yearnings. For Scorpios holidays are discovery journeys of the mind as well as the body. They completely immerse themselves in their quest for understanding of the deeper meaning of other cultures.

Traveling with a companion is quite agreeable with Scorpios, but it has to be someone who is not squeamish and easily frightened. Scorpios will visit haunted houses, damp, smelly dungeons and crawl into deep caves. They are master manipulators and will soon have their companions agreeing to their most bizarre suggestions. They will hardly ever book an organized tour. They aren't interested in the glitter and glamour of a place and will always go off the beaten track to discover what is hidden behind the bushes.

Scorpios have a burning desire to investigate all things unusual. Whatever exciting discoveries Scorpios make, they rarely divulge them to others, unless it can be exploited to their advantage in some way. An idyllic south sea island where there are unidentified plants and animals or the exact location of a rocky formation where the fossilized skeleton of a yet undiscovered dinosaur lies, may remain a Scorpio secret forever.

LOVE MATCH SCORPIO AND TAURUS

Although it is not immediately obvious and it may take a while to get up to speed, but Taurus' passion is just as impressive as Scorpio's. Though Taureans have the stamina to satisfy Scorpio their physical exploits are more conventional. Outside the bedroom there may be some strife as Scorpio is just as stubborn as Taurus and won't give in for the sake of peace. Scorpio is ruled by its many emotions and Taurus is ruled by practicality. Taurus may be somewhat stupefied by Scorpio's sarcasm. They share an affinity for accumulating wealth and the good life. Taurus may snort occasionally because of Scorpio's need for control, but will soon come to appreciate Scorpio's loyalty and strength.

Scorpios find the back alleys of their holiday destination much more interesting than the popular tourist spots. They rarely come to harm as it takes a brave soul to trifle with a Scorpio.

SCORPIO'S HUMOR IS BLACK...

...very black. People don't usually associate Scorpios with fun, which is a pity, because they have a highly sophisticated sense of humor. But it does have a slightly sinister and cynical undertone and is always very poignant. Scorpios have a gift for probing beneath the surface and are fascinated by the sinful side of human nature. The more forbidden a subject is, the more likely Scorpios will take a swipe at it. Nothing is taboo or too sensitive to make fun of. If it's macabre, perverse, controversial, or just plain evil, it will become the subject of the Scorpio pun.

Scorpios can hone in on a situation with surgical precision and their jokes nearly always have a subliminal message. Scorpios aren't squeamish either and it sometimes takes a strong constitution to stomach their humor. They will delight in describing a revolting situation to the tiniest detail and in the most colorful fashion. Many a friend has had to run to the toilet while listening to one of Scorpio's horror stories.

Adding a humorous slant to sensitive subjects, such as death, disease, religion and sexuality is a particular favorite of Scorpios. Though they will never resort to crude, obvious jokes, they truly delight in shocking people with their hidden suggestions. When everyone turns beetroot red, Scorpios will flash one of their devious smiles. If they have an inclination towards theatrics they can give a disturbing visual dimension to their humor.

Scorpios are the grand masters of sarcasm. No one is so skilled at this art of communication as Scorpios. They take great pleasure in exposing hypocrites, especially if they are high on the social ladder. Though they won't expose anyone who hasn't deserved it or can't defend himself or herself. Anyone hoping to have some fun at the Scorpio's expense should watch out. These people miss nothing and any verbal assault will almost certainly backfire. Scorpio's defenses are never slack and they are quick witted and will counter with lightning speed. Those psychological missiles have the power to destroy.

LOVE MATCH SCORPIO AND GEMINI

The complex Scorpio character fascinates curious Gemini, and
Scorpio finds the Gemini's vivacity irresistible. On a physical
level they are a terrific match in terms of passion and ingenuity.
Both are more than willing to try out all sorts of new ideas. But for
Gemini life is all fun and games and doesn't take it too seriously.
Scorpio's humor vanishes quickly when feelings are involved.
If Scorpio doesn't try to restrain Gemini too much and Gemini
takes the relationship a bit more seriously, they will uncover the
mysteries of the world and have fun doing it. Gemini will adore
Scorpio's black humor. It won't always be smooth sailing,
but it will be worth it and there will never be a dull moment.

With their powerful imagination Scorpios induce
a nightmarish scenario to their tales. Making fun
of frightening events could be Scorpio's way
of dealing with their own secret fears.

COME INTO MY BOUDOIR...

...said the spider to the fly. Scorpios seem to embrace the same sentiments when making love. They personify sexuality. It runs hot in their veins and seeps through their pores. Sex with Scorpios is not a just a physical joining of two bodies, it is an explosion of the senses, a torrent of passion gushing from the deep crevices of desire. There is no position they will not try and no fantasy wild enough to make them squirm. They'll be instigating all sorts of exotic love plays. They'll even be searching the libraries to find out how the ancient Greeks did it, or to discover some secret aphrodisiac used by a native tribe.

When Scorpios cast their eye on a potential partner, they will pursue them relentlessly until they've won them over. The pain of unrequited love does not discourage them. Quite the opposite is true, it will strengthen their resolve to succeed at all costs, even if they come to harm. Luckily for Scorpios, they seldom have to go to such lengths. Their natural sex appeal is so enticing that they rarely have to do more than use their magnetic gaze to lure the victim into their cave. Scorpios cast a spell over their partner and sex will never be the same again.

Making love with Scorpios is always associated with an element of danger. They take it all and will never be fobbed off with a faked orgasm or the excuse of a headache. If their attentions are spurned too many times Scorpio won't hesitate to look elsewhere for someone who appreciates their skills.

Despite their obsessive control, they are not selfish lovers. Scorpios are highly sensitive and will instinctively know how to loosen inhibitions. They give as much as they take. Scorpios want to bring their partners to unlimited heights of ecstasy and hold them there until the line between agony and pleasure is completely blurred. A sexual encounter with Scorpios is a union with the masters of sensual stimulation and there is a good chance that it becomes addictive. Scorpios don't want to just take possession of the body; they want the mind and the soul as well. Getting physical with Scorpios means total surrender.

LOVE MATCH SCORPIO AND CANCER

As water signs this is a highly emotional relationship.
Cancer craves security and domesticity, Scorpio wants power
and control. Scorpio's abundant passions will ignite passive
Cancer. Both have a tendency to sometimes jump to the wrong
conclusion where feelings are concerned, but the physical
attraction will ensure that arguments don't destroy the strong
emotional bonds. However, Scorpio won't accept Cancer's
fluctuating moods and may counter with some hurtful remarks.
Whereas Cancer won't like Scorpio's occasional outbursts
and volatility. Otherwise, Scorpio provides the strength and
protection and Cancer responds with deep love and devotion.

It is rumored that Scorpios have hypnotic skills
and are able to bewitch ordinary mortals
by the sheer power of their mind.

JUST A TOUCH POSSESSIVE

Marriage to the Scorpio is never easy. This sign is passionate to the extreme. When they love, they love with every fiber of their body. They give themselves completely and expect total devotion from their partners. Because of this absolute commitment they don't choose their life partner lightly. They will investigate all aspects of their intended's background; no stone will be left unturned, no secret uncovered.

For Scorpios the marriage vows are sacred. If their spouse is as committed as they are, Scorpios will never have a reason to stray and the marriage will endure all the pressures of time. Scorpios have a lot to give, but they also demand a lot. Their above average sensitivity allows them to tune into their partner's emotions with ease and their physical passions will only increase with the years. But Scorpios are not pushovers. If anyone does the manipulating, it will be Scorpio. There is only one way things are usually done in the Scorpio household, Scorpio's way.

It would be very unwise to dally with Scorpio's emotions. This sign senses deceit from a mile away and will not readily forgive a betrayal. When a Scorpio marriage turns sour it goes out with a gigantic bang. The pots will be flying as fast as the accusations. Everyone in the vicinity of a 500-metre radius will be privy to a sensational break-up. Hurt Scorpios become deadly. Just as they are able to love intensely, their dark side is equally powerful. Every sting has a long lasting effect. Once the damage is done and unpleasant things have been said, it becomes very hard for a Scorpio to kiss and make up. The emotional pain eats away at their souls and forgiveness is near impossible.

The Scorpio relationship is never boring. They love with such intensity that it hurts and can be jealous and possessive that it drives you crazy. Even a casual glance at someone else or coming home a few minutes later than intended can provoke the most terrifying scenes. If they could, Scorpios would lock their beloved into a golden cage, and some do exactly that.

LOVE MATCH SCORPIO AND LEO

A fixed water sign (Scorpio) and a fixed fire sign (Leo) will create some sizzling effects, both in a good and not so good way. One can see the steam rising when these two titans clash. Scorpio won't take kindly to being bossed around by Leo. These two have met their match as far as passion and temper is concerned. Scorpio will admire Leo's courage and ingenuity and Leo will value Scorpio's strength and loyalty. Scorpio must take care not to injure Leo's pride with sarcastic remarks about Leo's showmanship and Leo must curb the flirting with others so as not to unleash the infamous Scorpio jealousy. If they work together and Scorpio doesn't try to control Leo and gives the lion some freedom nothing will be impossible.

Scorpios are sensuous and passionate to the extreme. But they're also possessive, definitely have a jealous streak and may take radical measures to ensure the fidelity of their partner.

LOVES AN ODD MENAGERIE

As strange as Scorpios are, so strange will the pets be that they choose. Scorpios are strong individuals with a hankering towards anything unusual. You could find a tarantula named Charlie crawling over the kitchen bench top, a goanna called Lucy in the garden and a baby crocodile in the swimming pool. Scorpios are just as passionate about their pet snake and other creepy crawlies in their care as other people are about their pet dogs.

If Scorpios can resist the temptation to freak out the neighbors with a colorful array of obscure creatures and have chosen a dog, you can bet your lifesavings that it is an impressive breed. A trained Doberman is a perfect Scorpio dog. If Scorpios have a cat, it will most likely be a sleek, black cat with yellow, hooded eyes, which lurks in dark corners and has a stare that sends chills up the spine.

Scorpios are particularly sensitive to the needs of their pets. They train their animals in a firm, but loving fashion, always taking care not to destroy the animal's individuality. It is often fun to observe the odd characteristics Scorpio pets display. The Scorpio cat will probably use the toilet instead of the litter box and won't even forget to flush. It often appears that the animals will do anything just to amuse their Scorpio masters. Scorpios have a great capacity to love and they love their pets with the same intensity as they love people, maybe a tad more as they consider animals a lot trustworthier than some people. Once they have taken a shine to an animal, it doesn't matter what it looks like or how it behaves it will have a permanent place in the Scorpio heart and home.

Although they try to hide it, but Scorpios are really kind-hearted people, especially where helpless creatures are concerned. They will rescue an old three-legged cat from a dumpster, with a torn off ear and a large tumor sticking out from its tummy. They will take it home and lavish all their love and care on it. They will spend a fortune on veterinary treatment, just to make its remaining days more comfortable. When it has taken its last breath Scorpios will shed a few tears in private for the great courage of the little creature.

LOVE MATCH SCORPIO AND VIRGO

These two stimulate each other intellectually. However, restrained Virgo has some difficulty coping with Scorpio's physical demands, but otherwise the personalities mix well together. Neither is superficial and a deep commitment will develop. Virgo's passions are played out more in the mind than in the bedroom and Scorpio likes to mix the intellectual with the physical. Financial security and family matters are important to both. They work well together to achieve their goals and have no trouble accumulating wealth. This match is successful because they complement each other instead of competing. Virgo is a stickler for order and Scorpio just loves power, which Virgo is happy to relinquish.

Compassion and sensitivity are key Scorpio characteristics. When all others turn away, Scorpio is the one who will lend a helping hand.

LUCK OR SECRET POWERS ?

People born under the sign of Scorpio can sniff out opportunities of riches in the oddest places and situations. Is it just luck or are they in possession of strange powers that allows them to pinpoint the exact spot where a decent sized gold nugget lies three feet deep in the middle of the godforsaken desert?

Here is a person, who is not afraid of putting his or her money on an outsider. They will haunt the back streets of the city to see what is lurking behind the closed windows and who is fiddling at what in the garden sheds and cellars. They will find that young genius, who is putting together a clever invention in his garage and only needs someone to back him. Soon Scorpios will have the genius tied up in a watertight contract and start selling the idea to the world.

Scorpios are master manipulators and have no trouble imposing their wishes onto the market. With sheer willpower they will be influencing trends and can overcome the strongest opposition. If Scorpios believe in a project, they will bring it to fruition no matter what it costs. In pursuit of their goals, they walk over anything and anybody who stands in their way. Competitors or opponents hardly ever realize what Scorpios are doing until it is too late.

Scorpios rarely let their right hand know what the left is doing, much less take someone else into their confidence. Anybody asking too many questions and sticking their nose into matters that don't concern them will soon get an unmistakable warning to back off. Trying to trick Scorpio into revealing his or her intentions will never work because Scorpios can smell a rat a mile off. The only response they get is an icy stare.

For Scorpios having wealth is not as exciting as getting wealth. It is the testing of their skills, the matching of their wits against others, the psychological game of defeating an opponent and taking control of a situation that exhilarates Scorpios. This is the power that drives them to pursue more and more goals. Scorpios will risk everything, even their own lives, just to win.

LOVE MATCH SCORPIO AND LIBRA

Libra enjoys interesting people and Scorpio definitely fits the mould. Scorpio meets Libra's need for love and Libra will feel flattered by the jealousy trait. But Libra can't help the flirting and Scorpio won't suffer in silence. However, Libra is an expert in soothing the volatile Scorpio nature and will happily adjust, because nothing can come even close to the devotion, passion and excitement Scorpio offers on a daily basis. Outside the bedroom Libra helps balance and harmonize Scorpio's emotional turbulences, whereas Scorpio gives Libra some much needed focus and direction in life. Because each of their strengths is the other's weakness they complement each other perfectly.

Outward appearances never deceive Scorpios. With a deep understanding of their surroundings and an acute vision they can generate wealth from a seemingly valueless source.

SCORPIO'S HOUSE OF SEX

The Eighth House of the Zodiac deals with the quality of relationships, in other words, how we interact with one another and what we get out of a relationship. Since the ultimate interaction is the physical communion between two people, this house is commonly referred to as the House of Sex. Now anyone who is on intimate terms with a Scorpio will not be surprised that this sign rules the House of Sex. Scorpio and sex seem to go together like strawberry and cream. This sign is passionate about sex and there are no prizes for guessing as to which organs Scorpio also represents, of course, the sexual organs.

Naturally, an unruly romp in the hay is certainly something most Scorpios wouldn't object to, but you would be severely mistaken to assume that all Scorpios engage daily in wild sexual orgies. Though there are some that actually do exactly that, but you'd never know because Scorpios are always very discreet.

Although for most Scorpios frequency is important, it is really quality and not necessarily quantity that counts. In their view anybody can play the mating game. You don't really need much skill to achieve the basic purpose of sex and that is procreation. But for Scorpios the sexual union is so much more than just populating the world. It is a discovery journey of all the senses combined.

This house is about intimacy with oneself and another being, the opening of sacred chambers of the heart, soul, mind and body. The actual sex act can be symbolic for uncovering the hidden parts of the being. During sex one is mostly naked and this can also be seen as being 'naked' in an emotional and spiritual sense. Being without any clever clothing that hide our perceived physical faults as well as our innermost secrets and feelings, removing the restrictive barriers and letting go of the protections, gives us freedom to join and transform. This allows the true self to shine in perfection as well as imperfection. It is about giving, receiving and total acceptance.

The dynamics of our relationships with others and ourselves grow from within. Scorpios instinctively seek total freedom and a limitless sensual experience. They will invest all their energies to remove or at least stretch to breaking point those boundaries, which govern and restrict us. For Scorpios life is about evolving and creating new. And isn't that the ultimate purpose of sex – to evolve and create new?

In many cultures the sexual act is often associated with dying and rebirth and this again is a Scorpio trait. It is said that the Scorpio cycle of life is to die and be reborn again and again. Communion with another soul, either in a physical or spiritual manner, is like dying in bits and then being reborn in a slightly altered state. The Eighth House puts the stages sex, death and rebirth, where the body, the mind and the emotions become one, on the same level. It is a fluent transition from one stage to the next. Throughout our lifetime we experience the death of one thing and rebirth of another, be this in relationships, careers or beliefs, and of course our ageing journey. No one understands better than Scorpios that we are transient beings, constantly changing and evolving, dying and being reborn at the same time.

As passionate as Scorpios can be about sex they can also be very passionate about sexual abstinence. Sometimes the waiting and drawing out the anticipation heightens the senses and it is a way for them to practice that famous self-discipline. Some Scorpios even find as much sweetness in the agony of self-denial as in fulfillment.

But the Eighth House also represents support. This can either be financial, emotional, spiritual or physical support. Anyone who has ever been at the brink of despair may remember with fondness that it was actually a Scorpio friend who offered a helping hand. It is no coincidence that Scorpio is the sign gifted with an extraordinary insight. They sense when things aren't right and often provide support without the recipient ever knowing.

PLUTO: SMALL, BUT POWERFUL

Although Pluto has been demoted in 2006 to a dwarf planet, or to be more precise asteroid number 134340, in astrological terms it is still considered the "planet" which rules Scorpio. Pluto may be insignificant in size and its energy subtle, but its influence still packs a mighty punch. Maybe because it is on the outmost position of our solar system and the furthest from the Sun, where the darkness is at its blackest, that this "planet" was given the name of the mythical god of the underworld. Wherever Pluto reigns turmoil and upheaval are the order of the day and things can get ugly.

Pluto is about transformation, death and rebirth or regeneration. Since Pluto's discovery in 1930 the theory of reincarnation once more became popular. Pluto's personality is dark, sorrowful and extremely intense. When Pluto is involved pressures can build up rapidly and if no relief is found explode or implode. This can lead to strife, mental or emotional breakdowns, even death.

Since Scorpios are strongly influenced by Pluto they are often at the forefront of revolt and rebellion. At their best Scorpios will fight against injustice, oppression and bigotry. In their quest to create better conditions for all it often is necessary to use brutal force and Pluto gives Scorpios the emotional strength not to shy away from it. Under Pluto's influence destruction has a purpose. Only through death can rebirth come about, or in other words only by eliminating the outdated can the way be paved for progress.

No underworld is complete without its villains. If the dark side of Pluto gets the upper hand in Scorpios they can become involved in all sorts of illicit affairs and murmurings of connections to disreputable figures are heard. Pluto also governs crime, obsession, coercion, waste and other subversive activities. But the real purpose of Pluto is to entice its subjects to look underneath the covers, deep inside the soul to see what is there. Yes, this is scary and you may not always like what you see, but it is a necessary task in order to triumph in the struggle between good and evil.

SCORPIO BIRTHDAYS

24.10.1632	Antonie Philips van Leeuwenhoek, Father of Microbiology
25.10.1881	Pablo Picasso, Revolutionary Painter
26.10.1947	Hillary Clinton, Former First Lady, US Secretary of State
27.10.1728	Captain James Cook, British Explorer
28.10.1955	Bill Gates, Founder Microsoft
29.10.1947	Richard Dreyfuss, Actor
30.10.1960	Diego Armando Maradona, Argentine Soccer Player
01.11.1942	Larry Flynt, Publisher Hustler Magazine
02.11.1755	Marie Antoinette, Queen, beheaded French Revolution
03.11.1962	Marilyn, Rocker
04.11.1946	Laura W. Bush, First Lady to President George W. Bush
05.11.1941	Art Garfunkel, Singer
06.11.1955	Maria Shriver, TV Personality, wife of Arnold Schwarzenegger
07.11.1867	Madame Curie, Scientist, Discovered radioactive elements
08.11.1900	Margaret Mitchell, Author "Gone With The Wind"
09.11.1934	Carl Sagan, Professor of Astronomy
10.11.1483	Martin Luther, German Religious Revolutionary, Protestant Reformation
11.11.1974	Leonard DiCaprio, Actor
12.11.1929	Princess Grace of Monaco, Movie Star & wife of Prince Rainer of Monaco
13.11.1955	Whoopi Goldberg, Actress & Comedian
14.11.1948	Prince Charles, Prince of Wales
15.11.1945	Frida Lyngstad, Norwegian Singer, ABBA
16.11.1967	Lisa Bonet, Actress
17.11.1942	Martin Scorsese, Film Director
18.11.1962	Kirk Lee Hammett, Guitarist Metallica
19.11.1962	Jodie Foster, Actress
20.11.1925	Robert F. Kennedy, US Senator, assassinated 1968
21.11.1694	Voltaire, French Satirist
22.11.1890	Charles de Gaulle, French President